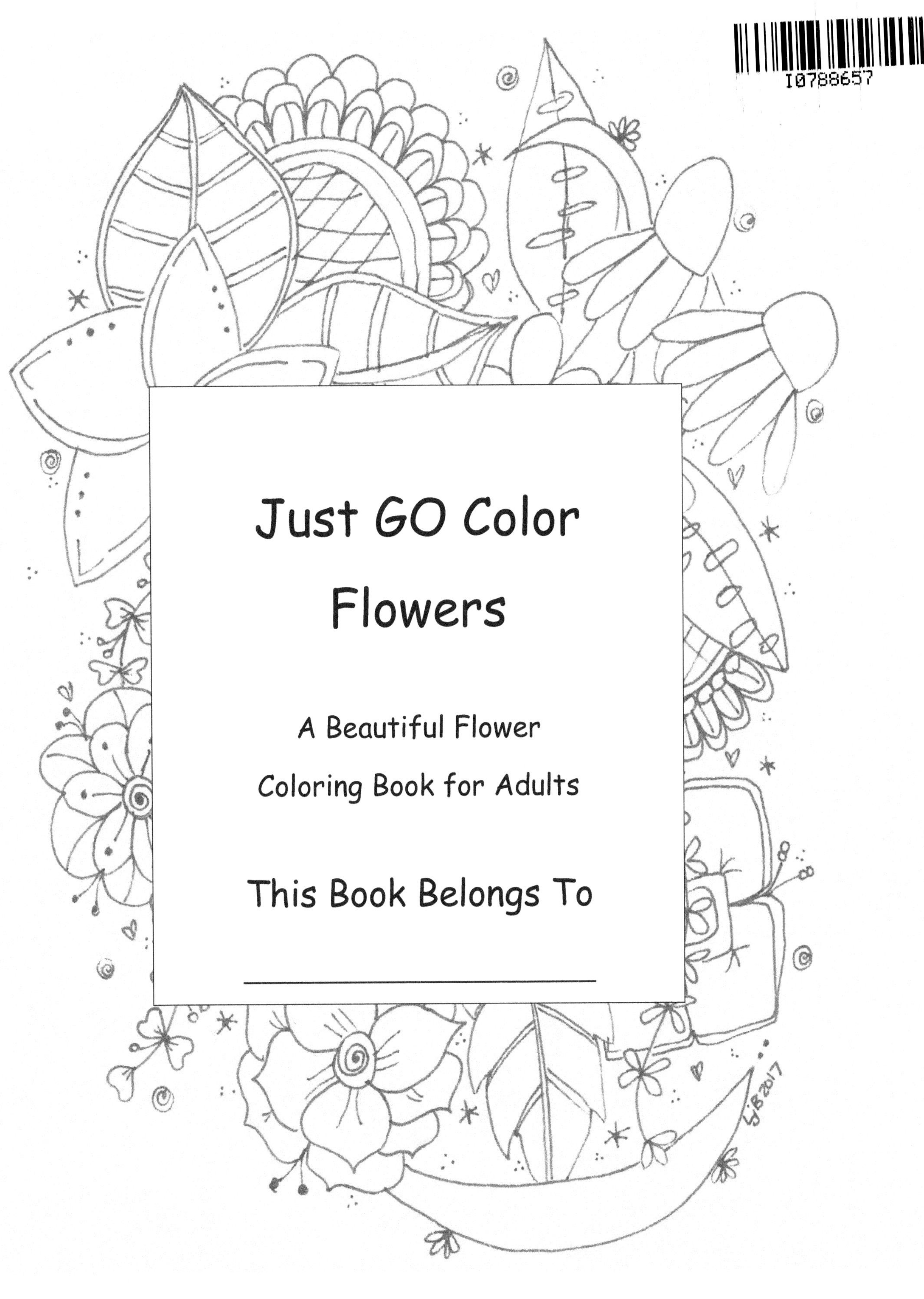

Just GO Color Flowers

A Beautiful Flower

Coloring Book for Adults

This Book Belongs To

____

Hello!

Welcome to the Just Go Color Coloring Book.

Coloring is a fantastic way to relieve stress and be creative or just zone out and be a kid again.

I designed each page so that you can add your own creative inspirations. You can add your own doodles and flowers and then tear the page out and frame it. Or color a page for a gift. I hope you will LOVE putting your own artistic touches to each design.

Please feel free to photocopy the designs for your personal use only. You might want to use crayons and then use markers. Or you may want to use a different color scheme. Or you may even want to copy onto watercolor paper and paint. I would love to see your work and my contact information is below.

If you enjoyed my Just Go Color coloring book, I would love for you to post a review on Amazon so that others can find it and enjoy it as you did.

Thank you so much!

Lori Bennett

ljbennett068@gmail.com

More titles coming soon!!

Trial Page

Try out your pencils, pens, markers, and techniques on this page.

If your coloring utensil is going to bleed through the page, simply place a piece of cardstock behind the page you are coloring. If you are using pencils and don't want those pressure marks on the next page, use the same technique of placing a piece of cardstock behind your design.

Colored by:_______________________________

Date:_______________________________

Colored by:____

Date:____

Colored by: ______________________________

Date: ______________________________

LJB 2017

Colored by: ____

Date: ____

Colored by: ____

Date: ____

Colored by: ______________________________________

Date: ______________________________________

Colored by:_______________________________

Date:_______________________________

Colored by: ____

Date: ____

Colored by:_________________________________

Date:_________________________________

Colored by: ____

Date: ____

Colored by: _______________________________________

Date: _______________________________________

Colored by: _______________________________________

Date: ____

Colored by:____

Date:____

Colored by: _______________________________________

Date: ____

Colored by: _______________________________________

Date: _______________________________________

Colored by:____

Date:____

Colored by: _______________________________________

Date: ____

Colored by: _______________________________

Date: _______________________________

Colored by: _______________________________

Date: _______________________________

Colored by: ____

Date: ____

Colored by:_______________________________________

Date:_______________________________________

Colored by: ____

Date: ____

Colored by: _______________________________________

Date: _______________________________________

About Lori…

Lori Bennett, the creator of Just Go Color, lives in Illinois in a small town of about 400. She has many different passions, which include her 5 wonderful grandchildren, the beach, and her family.

She gets her creativity from her grandmothers who were always working on some beautiful creation, and from her Mother who taught her to crochet.

She loves to visit her sister in Salt Lake City for a week each year and they usually find some craft to make that takes the entire week!

Lori works from home at her day job and creates in the evenings and on weekends. Her other artsy loves are crocheting, scrapbooking all the grandkids pictures, and quilting.

If she could, she would live on a beach, but for now the Midwest is home.